LIGHTNING BOLT BOOKS™

Pink Everywhere

Kristin Sterling

Lerner Publications Company
Minneapolis

Dedicated
to Ella

Lerner Publications Company
A division of Lerner Publishing Group, Inc.
241 First Avenue North
Minneapolis, MN 55401 U.S.A.

Website address: www.lernerbooks.com

Library of Congress Cataloging-in-Publication Data

Sterling, Kristin.
    Pink everywhere / by Kristin Sterling.
       p.   cm. — (Lightning bolt books™—Colors everywhere)
    Includes index.
    ISBN 978-0-7613-5440-6 (lib. bdg. : alk. paper)
    1. Pink—Juvenile literature. 2. Colors--Juvenile literature. I. Title.
  QC495.5.S7458 2011
  535.6—dc22   2009044814

Manufactured in the United States of America
1 — BP — 7/15/10

Contents

The Color Pink

Do you like sweet, pretty colors? Many people love the color pink.

Pink cotton candy is a popular treat at fairs and sporting events.

Look around you.
Pink is everywhere!

Pink can be found in nature. Beautiful roses grow in summer gardens.

Delicate cherry blossoms bloom on trees. They fill the air with a sweet smell.

This family is having a picnic under cherry trees full of pink blossoms.

Many things we eat and drink are pink. Look at this grapefruit. The flesh is pink and juicy.

Pink lemonade is a cool treat in hot weather. You can start a lemonade stand.

Lemonade can be pink or yellow.

Pink can be seen on animals too!

Flamingos lounge in shallow ponds.

Little piglets play on a farm.
They squeal and run.

These piglets are
pink and fuzzy.

People make and use
pink things. Some women
wear pink lipstick and blush.

Ballerinas twirl and leap in pink tutus and ballet slippers.

In ballet, this position is called passé.

Shades of Pink

There are many different shades of pink. Some are lighter, and some are darker.

How many shades of pink can you find in this girl's sweater?

Pastel pink is soft and light.
Baby Emily is wrapped in a
pastel pink blanket.

Hot pink is a loud, bright color.
Angel's cool sandals are hot pink.

Hot pink flip-flops and a beach ball are perfect for a bright summer day.

Fuchsia is a purplish pink color. Chloe rides in style on a fuchsia bicycle.

Chloe's friend wears salmon-colored glasses. Salmon is a pinkish orange color.

Tickled Pink?

People use sayings about the color pink. Maybe you have said them too!

Bobby was tickled pink when he won first place in a contest. That means he was very pleased.

Grandma Rose is in the pink. She is fit and feeling fine.

Paige Loves Pink

Paige is crazy about pink. It is her favorite color. She has fuzzy pale pink slippers and hot pink pajamas.

She loves strawberry ice cream.

It is her favorite treat.

Paige dresses in pink every day. She feels like a movie star when she wears her pink sunglasses.

Paige had a sleepover birthday party. Her pink teddy bear was there too!

Paige and her friends smashed open a pink piñata. Candy covered the ground!

Candy is stuffed into a piñata so that it will spill out when the piñata breaks open.

What do you think about pink?

Fun Facts

- The color pink can be created by mixing red and white paint.

- Crayola made the first pink crayon in 1949. It was called carnation pink.

- Baby boys used to be dressed in pink in the early 1900s. These days, baby girls are usually dressed in pink.

- Pink ribbons are symbols of hope for people with breast cancer. The ribbons were first given out in 1991 at a race for breast cancer survivors.

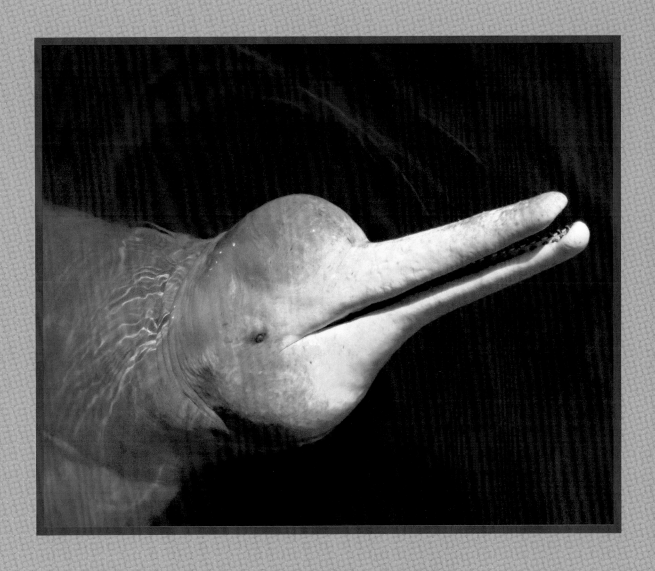

- Amazon River dolphins live in South America. These dolphins have pink skin!

- In a series of movies titled *The Pink Panther*, a clumsy detective searches for a famous pink diamond.

- You may have heard of a famous singer named Pink. Her real name is Alecia Moore.

Glossary

carnation: a type of flower

delicate: small and dainty

flesh: the soft, juicy pulp of a fruit

piñata: a decorated container filled with candy and gifts. It is hung from the ceiling to be broken with sticks by blindfolded children.

shade: the darkness or lightness of a color

shallow: not deep

Further Reading

Enchanted Learning: Pink
http://www.enchantedlearning.com/colors/pink
.shtml

Kann, Elizabeth, and Victoria Kann. *Pinkalicious.*
New York: HarperCollins, 2006.

McKee, David. *Elmer and Rose.* Minneapolis:
Andersen Press, 2010.

Montgomery, Sy. *Encantado: Pink
Dolphin of the Amazon.* Boston:
Houghton Mifflin, 2002.

Ross, Kathy. *Kathy
Ross Crafts Colors.*
Minneapolis:
Millbrook Press,
2003.

Index

Photo Acknowledgments

The images in this book are used with the permission of: © Ruthblack/Dreamstime. com, p. 1; © Blend Images/Alamy, p. 2; © age fotostock/SuperStock, p. 4; © Dfn-style/ Dreamstime.com, p. 5; © Mira/Alamy, p. 6; © Ulana Switucha/Alamy, p. 7; © Felinda/ Dreamstime.com, p. 8; © Tetra Images/Alamy, p. 9; © Skynesher/Dreamstime.com, p. 10; © Martinedegraaf/Dreamstime.com, p. 11; © Corbis Super RF/Alamy, p. 12; © Nancy Brown/Photolibrary, p. 13; © Photoeuphoria/Dreamstime.com, p. 14; © Okea/ Dreamstime.com, p. 15; © Cherylcasey/Dreamstime.com, p. 16; © Ginosphotos/ Dreamstime.com, p. 17; © Sweetthing/Dreamstime.com, p. 18; © Image Source/Alamy, p. 19; © Leonard McLane/Getty Images, p. 20; © George Shelley Productions/Getty Images, p. 21; © Image Source/Getty Images, pp. 22, 24, 25; © Nicholas Eveleigh/Getty Images, p. 23; © Walter B. McKenzie/Getty Images, p. 26; © Jean Glueck/Photolibrary, p. 27; © Elisabeth Coelfen Stills/Alamy, p. 28 (right); © Robynmac/Dreamstime.com, p. 28 (left); © Robert Harding Picture Library Ltd/Alamy, p. 29; © Digital Vision/Getty Images, p. 30; © Donn Thompson/Photolibrary, p. 31;

Front Cover: © Todd Strand/Independent Picture Service (background); © S-dmit/ Dreamstime.com (top left); © Pixelman/Dreamstime.com (bottom left); © Lazortech/ Dreamstime.com (top right); © Miflippo/Dreamstime.com (middle right); © Sqback/ Dreamstime.com (bottom right).